The Wonderful Wheel and Axle

Julie Murray

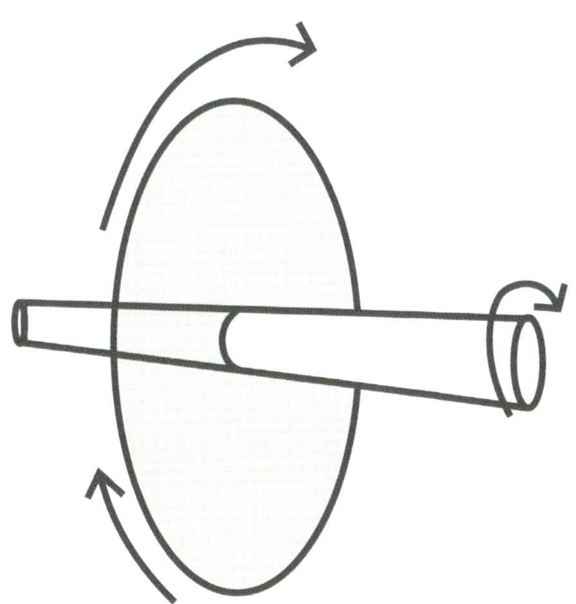

Abdo Kids Junior
is an Imprint of Abdo Kids
abdobooks.com

abdobooks.com

Published by Abdo Kids, a division of ABDO, P.O. Box 398166, Minneapolis, Minnesota 55439.

Abdo Kids Junior™ is a trademark and logo of Abdo Kids.

Printed in the United States of America, North Mankato, Minnesota.

052024

092024

Photo Credits: Getty Images, Shutterstock

Production Contributors: Teddy Borth, Jennie Forsberg, Grace Hansen

Design Contributors: Candice Keimig, Pakou Moua

Library of Congress Control Number: 2023948553

Publisher's Cataloging-in-Publication Data

Names: Murray, Julie, author.

Title: The wonderful wheel and axle / by Julie Murray

Description: Minneapolis, Minnesota : Abdo Kids, 2025 | Series: Simple machines | Includes online resources and index.

Identifiers: ISBN 9798384900641 (lib. bdg.) | ISBN 9798384901341 (ebook) | ISBN 9798384901693 (Read-to-me eBook)

Subjects: LCSH: Simple machines--Juvenile literature. | Wheels--Juvenile literature. | Axles--Juvenile literature. | Machinery--Juvenile literature. | Hand tools--Juvenile literature.

Classification: DDC 621.8--dc23

Table of Contents

The Wonderful Wheel and Axle

The wheel and axle is a simple machine.

wheel
axle

It is used to move things.

7

A wheel and axle is made up of two **cylinders**. These parts turn in the same direction.

axle
wheel

The inner **cylinder** is the *axle*.

The outer cylinder is the wheel.

axle
wheel

The wheel is larger than the axle.

wheel
axle

The wheel turns on the *axle*.

Force can be applied to the axle. The wheel turns quickly.

force

Force can be applied to the wheel. A stronger force is placed on the axle.

force
wheel
axle

The wheel and axle makes moving things easier!

Wheels & Axles Around You

drill

manual pencil sharpener

pizza cutter

windmill

Glossary

cylinder
a solid figure with a shape like that of a can.

force
power, energy, or physical strength.

Index

Visit **abdokids.com** to access crafts, games, videos, and more!

Use Abdo Kids code

STK0641

or scan this QR code!